COMING HOME

CRAIG RANDALL

switchboard
PUBLISHING

"That is my home of love: if I have ranged, like him that travels, I return again."

—William Shakespeare, Sonnet 109

INTRODUCTION

Home is an interesting concept when we take a step back and consider it. Truth is, most places I've never really felt at home. I think I understand why now.

I've lived in a lot of places in my life and have been a part of dozens of different communities trying to build exactly that: a *home*. But until recently, something never clicked. That's where this book came from. A book I couldn't be more thrilled to share with you.

I always saw home as a place. A place to rest, retreat, or recharge. A sanctuary to invite those you trust and love to. I don't think those ideas are wrong, by any means, just incomplete.

I've lived in various suburbs, the city, a small coastal town, and the college town that I now call home. In each place, I've built community (or tried to), had friends, hobbies, and various local functions to engage with. Overall, each phase of life was good. I look back on each with fondness; despite the hardships.

It wasn't until my family moved back from Amsterdam

at the latter end of the COVID pandemic that I started tackling what *home* really meant to me.

In a funny way, I felt more at home in Amsterdam than anywhere else. Another thing I understand better *now*. Many people in Amsterdam, those I interacted with, anyway, are expats. People outside their home. Removed from our old lives, for better and worse. And sometimes being removed from a situation can give you an incredible amount of perspective on it.

That's what moving abroad did for me. I could look back on my life; see it with so much more clarity. Distance will do that. Both the good and the bad. So, when I tried going off my anxiety medication and crashed, I had the luxury of time and space to dissect things during recovery. I was gifted with the incredible opportunity to retrace my steps—as I've mentioned before in the Introductions to *To Chase The Sun, Among The Wildflowers*, and *Rain Songs*. I got to see what went wrong; where and when it went wrong; and I caught glimpses of how to put it right.

As much as moving to Amsterdam triggered the growth I needed to branch out and face certain things, moving back from Amsterdam solidified everything and even created a much needed opportunity to face the initial instances of where various pains, traumas, or shame originated.

For the first time in my life, in Amsterdam, I cultivated a life where I felt a regular peace—med wash aside. Part of that, I came to realize, was the fact that some of the core conflicts in my life, things I'd left unresolved, didn't exist on that continent. But, if we were to move home, and proximity would have me interacting with them daily again, my peace would depend on one thing: *facing them.*

Living outside of my former context (one home) allowed me to see the patterns I'd built in life. In my youth, lacking the skills to navigate a situation, I'd run away. It's the quickest way to deal with the discomfort. And it's a very common human trait. The only problem is, while the immediacy of the discomfort is removed, in not facing it, we allow it to linger and fester, until it gets worse or most of the time explodes, having an altogether more negative impact on our life and the lives of those we love.

I'd come too far to let this happen to myself or my family, and hoping to mitigate as much collateral damage as possible, before moving home, I sat down and brainstormed a list of all the unresolved conflicts in my life.

It was scary, but powerful.

I narrowed it to ten things. Each one brought me a great deal of shame.

Something else occurred to me. I had a great deal more power in these situations than I previously realized. Most of them were relational. Friends or family, just relationships that had eroded over the years, because I or we lacked the tools to navigate them at the moment. But I'm gaining those tools now. And no situation is ever over until we decide–I told myself.

I planted seeds so when we arrived home, I could just start. I started reaching out. I messaged people; I brainstormed the desirable outcomes of situations. I worked hard to break down and understand my part in the situation. How it fell apart and how I could be part of the solution. It was thrilling.

The most incredible thing happened. Once we moved home, I started meeting with people. Running into them or sitting down with them through intention, and I faced what I had at first run away from, and resolution came. Not in every situation, but in enough of them. I rebuilt my response patterns, just like before when I'd rebuilt my mind, and I healed.

I would argue, I experience peace on a more regular basis here in the United States than I ever did in Amsterdam (a feat which feels extra incredible considering how much conflict exists in the US these days).

The journey's far from over, but as I mentioned, it's taught me a lot about the concept of home, the reasons I felt at home in certain places, not others, and why I feel more at home–right now–than ever before.

I have something I didn't before, in those other *contexts* and *homes*. Resolution. To the *big* things anyway. The things that either scared or hurt me when I was younger–some even as an adult––that I ran away from. Learning to turn back and face them. Lean into each situation's discomfort and grow. Experience resilience, and build a path out of the discomfort. This process led me to something more important.

Myself.

I found who I am, my capabilities, my genuine passions, the things that drive me, and how I like to spend my time. It makes perfect sense now, looking back, why I never felt at home in most situations before. I wasn't being *me*. I was being who I felt the context required me to be, or the people I'd surrounded myself with. How can a person feel at home if they aren't being true to themselves?

That's my takeaway. What I think this collection is about. The poems in these pages were written as I processed that journey of reconciling home. Of reconciling myself. In a way, every move I made throughout my life was another step in the search for a place I belonged, but it wasn't until I dug into the variable that mattered most that it clicked. The thing I took with me, each time, that never resonated. In all actuality, it would never work. *Me.*

I'm convinced now that's why I felt so at home in Amsterdam. I had left every context I'd known behind and was free to allow *myself* to ring through, and I'm certain I did. It was a wonderful and liberating experience.

But returning to each context? Standing in the strength of who I *really* am? Not bow down before anyone else's expectations? That's been one of the most extraordinary experiences of my life.

It ebbs and flows, like everything else, but is more solidified than ever before.

I'd like to leave you with the last poem in this collection. The poem that, to me, sort of culminates this journey. It's short, simple, and to the point, which I find helpful, but speaks to the search I think we're all on:

> *searching the world o'er,*
> *it has always been in you,*
> *the key and the door*

Thank you for reading. Here's to the peace we can each create!

Craig Randall
Corvallis, OR 2024

LEAVING, AND LEAVING AGAIN

Leaving

I used to think that doors
were only meant
for leaving;

For walking
through and never
looking back;

it's only recently,
certain things have got
me thinking,

perhaps, those
thoughts, like hinges,
are faulty--

and it's time they were replaced.

Houses and Homes

my heart split between
all the houses I've called home,
do I have to choose

With Fear

some masks reappear;
it's tempting for hearts t'give in
when h'bits drive with fear

Each Step

each step away
was a
lament

another cautious
choice that
confused

the difficulty is in
seeing the
ground
before
you

leap—and

hoping beyond
experience,
that after, all
the pieces still fit.

In Isolation

a tree can live in
isolation but will thrive
in certain forests

Tree Without A Forest

though still connected,
I can't help but feel a tree
without a forest

Rubble

look up and out,
clear the rubble from the path,
we can start again

New Shelter

sometimes its the storm
that saves, forcing us to seek
and find new shelter

Broken Shards

So much of what I thought I knew
I found to be untrue—

The way the world does wear itself,
Since placed upon the shelf—

To wait and wither if need be
Allows my heart to see—

I've circled back as time seemed right,
Holding thoughts up'o the light,

Whatever shadows that I cling,
Not to the future can I bring;

Our world, it longs for such release,
Not broken shards, but treasured peace.

Water Rises

water rises
all around, but equal
is my resolve

So Close, Somehow

to be so far yet
feel so close—somehow—within
my own heart, my home

Coming and Going

looking back, clutter's
all I see, wreckage to sift
through, and debris

Stale Fog

fog hangs stale o'er
still water, unsure whether
to cling or fade

Flames Climb

I struck the match,
allowed those flames to
climb,

with no thought to
past, present, or future, or
time;

not to feel—to numb—was
the only thought I had in
mind,

hence, the waylaid path
before me–scorched and
torn;

I burned the orchard and
cursed that fruit, for fear—*again*—of being
born.

Atlantic

thirty thousand feet,
the Atlantic underneath,
reconciling home

Sound Waves

oceans lie between
us now, tethered lines all cut;
will the sound waves reach

My Own Steps

my hand on
the wheel,
their foot on
the gas—

each turn, I
give way
a little more
than last—

my mind
less my
own—their grip,
tighter yet;

still,

I see
moments
to seize—and
orchestrate

my own steps.

Thin

skies grow thin
the higher that we travel,
dream of land below

FIRST INTERLUDE

Portland, Home Pt. 1

This bed of roses I was born,
I crawled and stumbled to a sprint;
Does birth beget our roots as sworn,
Do the initial homes we live imprint?

It's years since there my feet have tread,
Yet still my heart will beat for her;
It's years since there my paths have led,
Yet still my soul when there will stir.

Long have the years stretched ever on,
And other homes I've built now, since;
Though none as yet have crowned the dawn,
The search goes on from here to hence.

Always a piece, my heart you'll own,
Of all the homes I've ever known.

ARRIVALS AND LANDINGS

Walking Home With You

your hand in
mine,
walking
soundless
down
Each
road

the sidewalk
sings
to us;

my foot slips
but you catch
my arm, and

laughter
breaks
the
quiet.

Tender Frames

so brittle, their tender
frames crumble beneath my steps,
gentle autumn leaves

Be Baptised

let your roots grow deep;
brace for winter—be baptized
by the bitter cold

At Night, I Walk

at night
I walk,
steps stretch
into miles

the spaces between
buildings
expand;

at night
I walk
till the skies feel
fit to hold
my dreams;

at night
I walk
till hope seeds
in me,
my heart;

seeps
through my shoes,
into the road
beneath my feet;

at night,
dreams root
and fly—when
allowed—they

carry further
through the quiet,

settling bright;

each star is a sun,
each step, a hope,
and every footfall sings;

miles burn as dawn
inches close; the sky, light
and wide,

holds, sturdy,
catching and carrying
each dreamer as they fall
through

the night.

Momentum

why stop when
we have fuel
to burn,

when there's
so much to
explore,

so much to see
round those next
few turns,

see what
waits beyond those
next door.

Footfalls

each
pitter-patter
whispers to
me of your
hiding place,

"I found you!"

And Fly

I am
limited
only
by
my
fear to

fall

learn
trust. the
only
thing
that
I can
do:
is leap
is jump
is dive
is soar
is fall

...and fly.

Latitudes

The continents were
    shaped by time,
        molded,
            perhaps,
            with care,
            with rhyme.

What if the land could
    choose its course,
        to stay,
        to hold
            its place;
        stick to
            its source

Then, *perhaps* one
day I could, as well:
            besiege the dam,
            run it through
            and be
            un-hindered by

        such
      latitudes.

Take A Globe

take a globe,
or map,
and flip it

upside down,
or twist and turn

it all around,

any way
you feel is
right, to get

a better
view—maybe
then, at last,

I'll see me, and
you'll see you

To See the World

To see the world
wider than once
I had,

to learn
to grow
to love,

and thread the
sides of great
divide,

and hope
and push
and heal,

to find out who I really am
and, at last, to learn what's real.

SECOND INTERLUDE

Astoria, Home Pt. 2

A cozy corner, sea of sights,
the sweet and salty ocean air;
You were the place, and me the kite,
The place I learned to leap and dare.

Sometimes tree trunks can bear the weight,
Sometimes they give with too much strain;
I jumped too far, I knew too late,
But learned to listen from the pain.

In looking back, I see it now,
The lessons that you taught to me;
And better off, now, knowing how
To live and understand one's needs.

Always a piece, my heart you'll keep,
A home—years on—my soul still reaps.

DRIFTING

Unspoken

the deepest prayers
need not be spoken; heavy
hearts are understood

Fog

can't see past the fog
but still I step, trusting where
the path will lead

Retracing Your Steps

go.
will
you
where
out
figuring
so,
doing
in
been;
you've
where
out
figure
to
steps
your
retrace
to
have
you
sometimes,

Madness

it happened again,
and I ask myself: *when will
all this madness end*

Those Who Remind

hold tight to
those who remind you
who you are

Take Time

take time to

digest
the feelings and
assess

the
best
way

                                        forward.

Misconception

darkness, at times, can
be mere misconception,
mingled proof of light

Hearts Find Their Way Home

mustn't fear for those
we feel are lost; love lingers,
hearts find their way home

Thoughts

thoughts
at times

can skip
across

the space
of mind

like rocks
on water,

while others

clink, or sink, or drag—getting
lost in murky water.

For Clarity

hanging from the
bars, upside down,
brings a certain
clarity

as
all
the
world
itself

clings, scurrying

while
I swing.

Orbit Pt. 2

gravity,
a peculiar thing,
somehow
pulls me
back

somewhere,
mid-fall, it hits me,
I lost what
I lacked.

Break Chains

some don't understand
that forgiveness should absolve
and break chains, not revolve

Sing For

sing for those whose
silence overwhelms, for those
in need of hope

THIRD INTERLUDE

Corvallis, Home Pt. 3

A constant thread in life and heart,
A home—I wrestled with my grief;
A place I know I'll never part;
I came, cocooned, and found relief.

I walked your streets through every fall,
As autumn leaves do paint the streets;
A place to go whenever all
My other steps inferred retreat.

A place to land, lights always on,
A place that's always welcomed me;
A city, hearts who know will long,
A town to settle, sit and be.

Always my heart you will posses,
A home, a haven, place of rest.

ON THE ROAD

Reflection Lake

placid waters rest,
unmoved, out-willing the winds,
signalling us to sleep

Oak Tree

a single, small
oak tree hugs the highway's edge,
providing shade

Verna

winding roads to you,
cookies waiting for the boys,
childhood rekindled

Highway's Reach

the highway's reach is
long, longer even than my
thoughts which race along

Caffeine

caffeine's effect will
lose hold, gas up the truck,
make ready, hit the road

Tethered

with home behind yet
still ahead—my heart's tethered
to the road between

On The Road

the sky burns bright
over vast and endless fields,
morning on the road

Radio Tower

a lone radio
tower broadcasts 'cross the land
reaching only quiet

Underneath the Stars

driving underneath
the stars awakens something
old within these bones

Underneath Soft Evening's Light

driving underneath
soft evening's light, my weary
mind is quelled and soothed

The Open Road

driving, surrounded
by the open road reminds:
the wonder of this world

Lazy Towns

another lazy
town approaches, begging our
investigation

Enough Fuel

bad cups of coffee,
enough fuel to see us through,
adventuring with you

Sea Above

miles stretch on and on,
center lines strike the h'rizon;
the sky, a sea above

Outdated Maps

outdated maps and
no reception, nothing but
the will to drive

First Streaks

I'll stay up all night
with you to see those very
first few streaks of dawn

The Open Road Never Lies

alone with my thoughts,
the open road never lies,
guiding me on to truth

Brighter

stars, always brighter
in the mountains, reaching far
beyond each t'wering peak

PAST LIVES

City streets

these city streets still
sing to me the songs of youth,
of steadfast dreams

Upon the Lost

autumn leaves its mark
upon the lost, those who brave
forests without trails

Past and Future

standing on the same
street where past and future meet,
reconciling now

Those Streets

I wanna feel those
streets—once more—beneath my feet,
before it's time to flee

Each A Song

these old streets, they still
sing to me, each a different
youthful story and song

City Lights

when I close my eyes
I still see those city lights,
all their colored noise

Old Ghosts

revisiting my
old ghosts—remnants of myself
that I can now set free

Comfort Comes

comfort comes as my
feet tread 'pon those paths of past,
'pon familiar fields

Monuments

memories are
monuments of what has come,
be sure t'frame with care

Cathedrals

let's build cathedrals
with all we've left behind,
paying homage to the trail

Outrun The Past

can't outrun the past,
might as well lean in to *now*,
make this moment last

Shifting Tides

tides will always shift;
their beauty, such consistent
inconsistency

Curbs and Streets

these curbs and streets, the
same cracks since I was sev'nteen;
the stories each hold

FOURTH INTERLUDE

Amsterdam, Home Pt. 4,

Opportunity, she will sing,
Calling loud, we cannot ignore;
So blindly leap, to see what brings
The crown of all movements before.

Those city streets both old and worn,
Cobbled along canals entwined;
The true first place my heart was torn,
The beauty held so hard to find.

I found cover, a home to heal,
To grow and stretch and become whole;
A place where hope would become real,
A place where fear did flee the soul.

Always a piece, you have my heart,
Despite the needs one must depart.

RETURNS

Returning

I see it now,
the way they were
designed, and why;

locks and hinges,
each edge carved
for perfect fit,
so we will
walk inside,

return from whence
we thought we
had to leave

and seek those parts of
self we left behind.

Yearn for Home

my heart yearns for home,
a touch of familiar,
to feel un-alone

Lost The Sun

I may've lost the sun,
but cling to memories that
will guide one's heart home

Circling

circling, I've been
searching wide and far for such
a place to land

Maintenance

like all good work
we must put in the time,
maintenance of the mind

Another Rain

another rain
came, weakening
the soil,

certain parts,
rough, near the edge,
jagged;

I see now,
it needed softening.

Tribute To The Young And Old

The young have need to watch the morning rise
Not pave the night with life and feel the moon;
For those who witness dawn unfold are wise.

The heart of youth is to seek their sleep's demise,
To live and be and know what's gone too soon;
The young have need to watch the morning rise.

With age the slowing calm comes as surprise,
And rest becomes to them life's sweetest boon;
For those who witness dawn unfold are wise.

No context yet for dreams they will devise,
Nor sense for songs sung in a gentle croon;
The young have need to watch the morning rise.

For youth, when looking back, is but a guise,
As flames unfold, softening night's tune,
For those who witness dawn unfold are wise.

There is a time in life to miss the runes,
To sprint and not to bask the skies of june;
The young have need to watch the morning rise,
For those who witness dawn unfold are wise.

Tangled Roots

let those roots tangle
and converge–digging deeper,
heart and home will merge

Kindles Conversation

the open flame
kindles conversation well
into the night

Old Adage

old adage rings true
so I click my heels and say,
"there's no place like home"

Needful Reminder

needful reminder
for those times you're plagued with doubt:
you have what it takes

Different

different
trees each take on
their own form
of bark—
of leaf—
of stem —
and root—
yet they share
this commonality:

each will weather storms.

Testaments

memories,
stories woven from
where we once stood;

they exist for truth,
reminders;

things we
mean to tell
ourselves

somewhere down the road.

Weary Hearts

home is where we
feel the most at peace, where
weary hearts find rest

A Forest

a forest thick, with
deepest roots, fends itself best
from isolation

Leaning Into Loss

leaning into loss,
grief is the recognition
that what's gone was good

Quiet Connection

water boils,
two cups sit waiting to steep,
quiet connection

At Last, Be Free

The land, it opens far in front of me,
Expanding—reaching to the mountains and the sea;
Allowing for our hearts to at last be free.

The road, it calls, it leads and bids me flee,
All that slows and weighs me down—I need r'prieved;
The land, it opens far in front of me,
Expanding—reaching to the mountains and the sea;

The waters carve each valley to receive
Both prayers and lamentations, life concedes,
At least the skies are constant with their needs;
The land, it opens far in front of me,
Expanding—reaching to the mountains and the sea;
Allowing for our hearts to at last be free.

Drink Deep

each tiny flake falls
threading magic through the air;
rest and breathe, drink deep

Leonard Pt. 2

I'll try to be good
but if I can't, then as you
said: *I'll be like you*

Looking Back

looking back reminds
of what love has overcome,
reasons to give thanks

Beauty Surrounds

remember
how beauty surrounds and
live in awe

Loss and Gain

We are like the seasons in that we change,
At first, we're born, we bloom, we hold the reins,
Each of us a story of loss and gain.

The first full leaves will always think it strange,
Let nothing past the morning's sun lay claim; still
We are like the seasons in that we change,

By midday, in heavy heat our ripeness wanes,
Already songs of early evening crane—thus,
Each of us a story of loss and gain.

Hues will turn as green will fade to gray
But we may see such beauty if we may, for
We are like the seasons in that we change,

Youth, a gift we learn to never hold in vain,
As wisdom teaches one: *lean into pain*;
We are like the seasons in that we change,
Each of us a story of loss and gain.

Rising

come, rest on my
shoulder; let strength gather
through our mingled tears

Dinosaurs

pretending to be
dinosaurs with you—hunting
through the house, our home

A House For Grief

set your burdens free,
hearts are made for movement not
as a house for grief

Warmth And Light

the weakest flames
still give off both warmth and light,
hope enough for all

I Sink Into the Softness of the Night

I sink into the softness of the night,
The deepest rest, I've found upon these shores;
Such sleep is where I go to claim the light.

When day is done and seeks its own respite
I rest my head, my mind, as to restore;
I sink into the softness of the night.

Beneath the starlit fields that shine so bright,
I drift off to dreams, to worlds that I adore;
Such sleep is where I go to claim the light.

For years, these hours brought me only fright,
For fear of keeping up until the morn;
Now, I sink i'to the softness of the night.

As habits form, habits they can be made right,
Tired, I grew, of seeing night with scorn;
Now, sleep is where I go to claim the light.

It took years to let go all that came b'fore,
Years t'build this path that leads to what's in store;
To sink into the softness of the night;
To sleep, where now I go to claim the light.

Hope Remains

even forgotten,
hopes remain; the truest seeds
hold for brighter days

The Trick

the trick: learning to
listen to the pain, letting
it lead you to peace

Tomorrow Beckons

that frail line upon
the sea's edge—holding
up the sky;

dreams are
made of this same strength,
imbues belief to thrive

so what to choose
when tomorrow beckons us,
like the sun:

I'll rise.

Making Way

feel hope in each drop
that falls, softening the soil,
making way the path

An Open Sky

everything is an
open sky for those whose hearts
have healed with time

The Key And The Door

searching the world o'er,
it has always been in you,
the key and the door